If You Don't Say It Now

Finnegan Fields

Presentation by *BookLeaf Publishing*

Web: www.bookleafpub.com

E-mail: info@bookleafpub.com

ISBN: 9789357447584

First edition 2022

DEDICATION

For Aaron.

I love you. I miss you. I am so sorry.

Rest easy, Cupcake.

black & white

i don't remember the day it ended. i don't remember the conversation. i don't remember the fight.

i remember pretending it was easy. i remember ignoring all of the ways that i hurt him. i remember soaking my grief in bitterness until i could no longer recognize my misery. i remember choking at the sound of his name and exploding on anyone who dared to mention him. i remember hating him in all of the ways that i did not want to hate myself.

it's easy to hold onto a bad memory and use it to paint over years of good ones. it's easy to use black and white to cover the grey. it's easy to use anger to become stone.

on a long enough timeline, the anger dissolves. what remains is more sadness than what you started with. you realize that the hate wasn't hate at all, it was just sadness with nowhere to go.

if you don't say it now, #1

i wanted to write about a beautiful first love. i wanted to take a tragic ending and turn it into something hopeful. i wanted this love to be poetic.

i wanted to write about the innocence. your hands wrapped in mine while we talked about a beautiful and peaceful future.

there is not enough artistic flare in the world to change our reality.

we had a beautiful first love and i destroyed it with my bare hands. i do not know how to turn that into poetry.

conversations we had before you left this world

"we're going to die some day, you know. and that makes me very sad."

"don't be silly, baby girl. we aren't going anywhere."

"we all die. and when we do, i'll miss you so bad."

"we'll always be together. i love you. you and i will be together forever."

if you don't say it now, #2

to live in this body is to constantly hear the ticking of a bomb.

an alternate ending where i did not ruin us

in this story, we are adults making pancakes on a sunday morning. we laugh about our stories of a reckless youth.

the kettle starts to whistle and the sun shines through our window. this is it. this is what we were waiting for all of those years.

in this story, i didn't set fire to the world around me. i didn't self destruct and make you pay for the damages.

in this story, what i have is beautiful and what i loved isn't gone.

if you don't say it now, #3

there is a strange beauty in destroying yourself to be remade.

burn yourself to the ground and rebuild from the ashes.

be desecrated so you can be rebuilt.

lie to yourself and say that this destruction matters.

make this pain worth it.

what i should have said

i am sorry. i am sorry.

please forgive me.

regret isn't a strong enough word

i found out you died from a facebook message
i collapsed to my knees
i hoped it was a cruel joke

a decade spent swallowing my shame
within a moment, it clawed it's way from my
mouth
sat down in front of me
and has been staring me in the eyes ever since

i wish i was kinder while you were here
i wish i had apologized for all of the things that i
never did
i wish i had apologized for all of the things that i
did do

i have apologized to the stars more times than i
can count
i have cursed the universe for taking you away

because i am here, and you are gone, and i only
have this pen and this paper
i will say just this

thank you
thank you for showing me what love really is
thank you for being the calm center of the
universe when my soul was on fire
thank you for being the only star in the sky on
many nights
thank you for being my world of firsts
thank you for holding my hand as we grew up
thank you for being you
thank you for everything

if you don't say it now, #4

i have never said goodbye and meant it.

ana, my dear friend

ana showed up unannounced
when my insides could not stop screaming, she
promised to give me control
ana would be my calm in this crazy world

slowly, ana carved away everything but bone
mirrors become our enemy
she tells me that everything is going according
to plan
i believe her

we are always cold. always dizzy. always tired.
lunch invites are never accepted and i haven't
seen the beach in years
ana tells me that this is the cost of having
command over your life

ana is a friend i've outgrown but don't know how
to say goodbye to
letting go of her means letting go of everything
we have accomplished together
all of the praise and compliments
"i'd die to look like you," they say

i'd die to look like me, too

if you don't say it now, #5

i don't know how to exist unless i am an object
of desire
i take my clothes off
in a car
at a park
at a party
anywhere that i am asked

i hear boys don't like it when you say no
so i never do

i meet a boy who loves me and writes me music
i lie and say i cannot stand him
i leave to visit a boy who only sees me after
midnight

i meet a boy who is smart and makes me laugh
i meet a boy who makes me forget all of the bad
in the world
i leave without saying goodbye

i find a boy i want to spend my life with

i love him too much
i walk out the door and do not look back

i start dating a boy who i do not love
when he leaves, i will not be sad

my love exists only in memories
untouched
safe from being ruined by the world and it's
nasty tricks
if anyone is going to leave, it's going to be me

i see you

for the women who were called beautiful before
they were called brave
called pretty before they were called powerful
complimented on their clothes before they were
complimented on their courage

darling, you are magnificent
you are resilient
you are strong
you are made from everything that they could
not take from you
you are more than words can express

i see you

i see you

i see you

family values

in my family, love and abuse are synonymous.

i am told a man would not react strongly if he
did not love you.

the boy throws my belongings in the yard. i pick
them up and ask to come back inside to
apologize.

when told i am unlovable, i promise i will
change and i beg to stay.

five days after he leaves me black and blue, my
grandmother says i should have forgiven him by
now. as if my lack of forgiveness is the problem.

the women in my family die holding hands of
men that only know how to break their heart.

in my family, women take the scraps that they
are fed and call it a meal.

if i should have a daughter, this is what i will tell
her.

in our family, we love our women fiercely.

in our family, boundaries are indestructible.

in our family, we listen to our bones when they
tell us to run.

dinner talk

at the restaurant table, as if he was bringing up
the weather
he tells me that he loves me, but he hates how
sad i get
he tells me that he can't pour his love into
someone who doesn't feel it the way he wants
them to
he tells me that i do not think of him enough on
my bad days
he tells me that i need to work harder to make up
for these shortcomings
he tells me if i loved him, i would not make him
deal with my depression

he has the nerve to ask me why i haven't been
able to finish my dinner

if you don't say it now, #6

it's not that you didn't feel bad
but you never felt bad enough for it to matter
guilt is a futile emotion

always

we are on a park bench at midnight. you play guitar and sing my favourite songs. i loved you then.

we are moving to a new city. i'm not nervous with you by my side. i loved you then.

i tell you my secrets and expect you to leave. you tell me everything will be okay. i loved you then.

i am afraid of my own feelings. i tell you we need some time apart. you didn't believe me, but i loved you then.

i see you years later. you have smile lines that only make you more endearing. you tell me that you've found happiness - i don't dare to ruin it. god, did i ever love you then.

one day, i will be older and wiser, reminiscing on those i loved when i was young. i will think about the chances i didn't take and i will hope that you are happy. i will still love you then.

if you don't say it now, #7

"how do you love someone without giving them the power to destroy you?" she asked.

"you don't," he said, "love is giving someone your heart and hoping they'll at least be gentle."

the door is unlocked

i do not know you yet.

when we meet, i will welcome you with open arms.

i will trace the freckles on your skin and listen to all of the stories of how the world tried to break you but couldn't.

i will put down all of my weapons.

i will make a home for you here.

www.ingramcontent.com/pod-product-compliance
Lightning Source LLC
LaVergne TN
LVHW051252200726

843510LV00011B/1808